NONSENSE

by Barry Rudner

Illustrated by Thomas Fahsbender

Watercolor by Peggy Trabalka

ISBN 0-925928-04-6

Printed/Published in the U.S.A. by Art-Print &
Publishing Company. Tiny Thought Press is a trademark
and service mark of Art-Print & Publishing Company.
Publisher is located in Louisville, Kentucky
@ 1427 South Jackson St. (502) 637-6870 or
outside Kentucky 1-800-456-3208

Library of Congress Catalog Card Number: 90-83542

In memory of B. Bettelheim

There once was a lady
who lived in a park,
with no place to go
or sleep after dark.

She ate a hot meal
when she was able.
A garbage can top
was used as a table.

Thrown away cartons
were used as a home.
When they wore out,
again, she would roam.

2

One day in this park
she saw a young boy.
His feet dragged along.
His steps lost their joy.

For while the boy slept
between evening and dawn,
this boy woke to find
his humor was gone.

Something was missing.
He looked in the mirror.
An upside down smile
was all to appear.

He growled out the door.
The boy snarled at the day.
He barked at his dog
as it came up to play.

The boy with no smile
then looked up to see,
the lady with nothing
smiling with glee.

"Who are you," he asked,
"that you smile as you do,
when all that you have
you carry with you?"

6

"I'm the Duchess of Silly,
the Madam of Mirth,
and this is my kingdom,"
she said from her berth.

7

She made herself laugh.
She fell back in her seat,
until all he could see
were the tops of her feet.

The boy with no smile
just stood there confused.
He quietly said
in a voice unamused.
"Your cane is no scepter.
This bench is no throne.
Your subjects are pigeons.
Your crown jewel a stone.
So how can you sit there
and laugh and make gags,
when all that you have are
some brown bags and rags?"

"Whatever," she answered,
"that I have not got.
I have got something
you truly do not.
It cannot be measured
in dollars and cents.
It is richer than gold.
It is utter nonsense."

"Nonsense?" he asked.
"Is that what I've lost?
Wherever it is must
be found at all cost!"

The Duchess then giggled
and laughed in her sleeve.
For somehow she got
the boy to believe,
that she had the cure
to heal his long face,
by sending the boy
on a wild goose chase.

13

"Maybe," she said,
"it is not lost at all.
And you left it at home,
in your room or the hall."

"Or maybe it's there
and it merely won't start.
It might just be flat,
or you need a spare part."

14

"Maybe it's stolen
and you need a detective.
Or maybe it's broken
and it's only defective."

"Could it be," she asked,
"that it strayed like a pet?
Maybe your nonsense
was lost like a bet?"

15

"Maybe it's lost
like half of your shoes,
one sock of a pair,
or a dare that you lose."

"Maybe you threw it
away by mistake.
Or maybe your funny
bone has a break."

"Thanks," said the boy,
as he ran off to see,
if he could find
his lost sense of glee.

The boy with no smile
searched store after store,
but all that he heard
were some shopkeepers roar,

"You're funny," they said
to the boy one by one.
"We think you have found
your lost sense of fun."

Place after place
that's all the boy heard.
But the boy with no smile
did not feel cured.

"Nonsense," he said.
"So what did I say
to make them all laugh
and giggle that way?"

He walked away slowly.
He did not understand,
why everyone laughed
with their belly in hand.

He sat on the sidewalk,
as cold makes one huddle.
He stared at himself
in a mirror clear puddle.

He looked in the puddle
and saw a huge grin.
The boy felt a tickle
from somewhere within.

He rocked back his head
and shortly thereafter,
the boy felt the joy
and the air filled
with laughter.

23

The boy's sense of humor
was not ever broke.
He never had lost it.
It was simply a joke.

The boy looked no further
and all became clear.
He ran to the Duchess
to share the good cheer.

"I see," said the Duchess,
"you found what you sought.
It never was lost
in a place that you thought."

"My search," said the boy,
"was never in miles.
Nonsense is found
where we wear our smiles."

25

He thanked the Duchess
for what she had done,
for helping him find
his lost sense of fun.

The boy with a smile
then laughed with delight.
He applauded the Duchess.
His smile shined bright.

They giggled and laughed
as they sat in the park.
They chortled and chuckled
until it was dark.

For now the boy knows
if it happens again,
the smile that he wears
can be his best friend.

About the Author ...
Barry Rudner was born in Detroit where
he can still be found to be growing up.

About the Illustrator ...
Thomas Fahsbender is a sculptor from
New Preston, Connecticut who has never found
a comfortable pair of dress shoes.

About the Publisher ...
Art-Print & Publishing Company (Tiny Thought
Press) would like to hear from
you. Please call us at 1-800-456-3208
and tell us what you think about
"Nonsense." We are committed
to the enjoyment of children, parents
and grandparents alike.

Other Tiny Thoughts at Local Stores . . .

The Littlest Tall Fellow

The Bumblebee and The Ram

The Handstand

Will I Still Have To Make My Bed in the Morning?